An Angus&Robertson Publication

Angus&Robertson, an imprint of HarperCollins *Publishers*

25–31 Ryde Road, Pymble, NSW 2073, Australia
31 View Road, Glenfield, Auckland 10, New Zealand
77–85 Fulham Palace Road, London W6 8JB, United Kingdom
10 East 53rd Street, New York NY 10022, USA

First published in Australia in 1995
Copyright © Helen Glisic 1995

National Library of Australia
Cataloguing-in-publication data:
Glisic, Helen, 1963–
Spellbound
ISBN 0207 186413
1. Magic. 2. Rites and ceremonies. 3. Charms.
4. Incantations. I. Title.
133.44

Design by Liz Seymour
Photography by Brett Odgers

Printed in Hong Kong
95 96 97 98
5 4 3 2 1

SPELLBOUND

HELEN GLISIC

Angus&Robertson
An imprint of HarperCollinsPublishers

DEDICATION

I would like to dedicate this book to all my teachers, both past and present,
and to those who are on their own magical path.
To Bronwyne Adams, thank you F.B for all your loving support,
and to Merlin who was always there for me. To all my other friends
who listened, encouraged and supported me through the writing of this book,
and to my family, thank you. A special thanks to
all the Wild Women of the South—Red Feather.

LOVE AND LIGHT,
HELEN.

contents

GIFTS OF TH

acred Chamber Dream Diary Natures Life Force Cast

Introduction

'Magic is the space between knowing it works and wanting to know it works.'

Magic is the gift of love from our source and creator. It is given to us to be used to improve our everyday existence. Magic is a part of our daily life and we need only look around to be made aware that everything we do is based on magic and rituals. The way in which we came into being is a wonder in itself, and demonstrates that magic has been part of the world since time began.

People today view magic as merely fantasy or make-believe. The word 'magic' conjures up half-forgotten childhood tales of adventure, splendour, wishes granted, and quests for dragons that have all been safely put away. Or have they? Some of us only ever visit the world of magic in our imagination and dreams, where magic can always be found. By keeping in touch with our inner world of wonder we can re-experience the feeling of finding a bottle with a genie in it. We need magic now more than ever if we are to open ourselves to windows of endless possiblities. The experience can be life-changing. Where there is imagination, there is magic.

In earlier times, people simply believed in the existence of magic as it was important for their survival. They lived in communities and magic was a part of their community life, it was an everyday communion with nature. Magic was, and still is, the natural universe working in harmony with the human spirit and the physical body.

Magic is not just for those who are lucky, although luck will play whatever role you want it to in your life. You yourself are, ultimately, the reason that magic works. Together with a few tools that are charged with the energy of your intention, you will be able to make magic work for you.

When magic is respected it can only be used for the good of all. Magic should never be used to manipulate another person without their permission, even in a positive way, as each person is responsible for themselves. When we use magic for the positive, our lives can only be enriched and made happier.

Magic was once used mainly for healing the spirit, but it can also provide each person with practical solutions to everyday problems, such as how to protect your home from unwelcome guests (even from your mother in law!), while giving you tools for creating a loving environment in your home or office. The difference between powerful magic and mere wishful thinking often depends on how skilfully you can alter your consciousness by focusing your intention on your needs.

This book is designed to give you, the reader, a look into the world of magic and its role in your everyday life and to see yourself through new eyes. What awaits you are the rituals, spells and blessings of antiquity and today, which have been tried and tested by myself and others. Some spells are from old folklore traditions, although most have been formed from my own personal experiences. These latter have been created from working in and on my life, or have been inspired by my interactions with other people and the way in which others have used magic often without being aware of it. When people use magic unawares, it enriches their life as well as the lives of those around them.

By the end of this book you will know the names of the various tools used in magic, and most importantly you will know how to develop your own magical traditions which can be used time and time again. Always remember to follow the first rule of magic: harm no-one.

Information found in these pages is for those wishing to gain an understanding of how each individual is responsible for creating their own reality. The magic held within each person does not require a knowledge of ancient ways or worship of any gods other than the God/Goddess within. I personally do not belong to any group, and have my own way of understanding what I hear and read, while making it fit in with my own beliefs. I encourage each reader to take what they need and make it their own. Do only what feels right for you. If in doubt call on the love in your heart to guide you.

Some of the spells, rituals and blessings need careful preparation, others merely serve as a reminder of how simple magic can be. Read through the instructions carefully before attempting any ritual or spell.

Join me on a journey to a place visited only in your imagination and dreams. You will bring back with you some new and interesting ways to make your life more magical and enchanting. Sit comfortably on your magical carpet and slip into your magical cape, but make sure you have room to bring back some magical goodies.

Away we go to enter the enchanted forest of dreams. Let me warn you that the journey will not be without a little self discovery.

Use what you find in this book to create a more loving environment for all to see and feel.

At the end of this book there is a list of books that I have recommended along with a list of suppliers of the various ingredients mentioned. Please write to me and tell me of your magical journey, so we can compare notes, and bring more love and magic to our world.

SO MOTE IT BE

'I will not deny you anything, only you can do this.'

Please note: Do not perform rituals, spells or blessings under the following conditions:

- ☑ WHEN YOU ARE FEELING ANGER AT YOURSELF OR OTHERS
- ☑ IF YOU ARE UNWELL OR EMOTIONALLY UPSET
- ☑ IF YOU ARE UNDER THE INFLUENCE OF ANY FORM OF DRUGS, EG ALCOHOL

A NOTE ON MAGIC

The most frequently asked question by people is 'Does it work?'. I can only say that when you believe in yourself and focus on a positive outcome, and you are able to establish your needs without a doubt, then it will work. If you feel that the magic does not work, the reason is usually because the desire is often masqueraded as a need and in magic a desire is not enough to warrant your expected outcome — there must be an all-encompassing need for you to receive what you most want. Always create magic with an open heart and allow the love to bring you your wish.

What is Magic?

☑ An art of influencing events by controlling nature or spirit

☑ The ebb and flow of the ocean, the wind that blows the trees, held within the unopened rose bud, a falling star, the sound of the ocean in a shell

☑ The art of causing changes to occur consciously, where humans may rise above their everyday consciousness to fulfil their spiritual potential

☑ The practice of causing change by using powers as yet not defined or accepted by science

Magic is a natural practice and many of us use it without conscious awareness. The basic practice of magic is to exercise influence over one's environment with the help of tools. Magic is a combination of the use of herbs, oils, symbols, visualisations, affirmation and personal focus.

Visualisation refers to creating images in your mind to bring about a positive outcome and then using that image as a manifestation of your wishes. Affirmation is the power of spoken words used in a positive manner to change negative beliefs. Personal focus is the strength of your intention, your level of concentration and just good old-fashioned faith in yourself.

Magic is therefore based on natural elements working in harmony for the good of all, using the subtle energies of herbs and nature. These energies flow to and from the person working the spell or ritual, into the tools being used, such as candles, crystals, stones and symbols. These energies are then transformed by you as the practitioner, from your wisdom within, through the power of visualisation and affirmation. Energy directed in a focused way is life-changing and magical.

Connecting to the rhythms and cycles of the earth will bring us back into balance with nature. Ceremony is one way of creating that connection with the earth. The knowledge of this fact is the reason why magic has been kept alive in ancient cultures and is now being used by many people to reconnect to, and to commune with, the natural world.

TYPES OF MAGIC

There are many different types of magic. The three main types are White magic, Black magic and Earth magic. One could enter into all kinds of debates over this topic, however I will simply describe what each type of magic means to me, as each individual will have their own interpretation.

White magic is the use of natural forces and spiritual realms. It is a way of life for many people that involves meditation and exploration of the elements of the self. This relates to one's beliefs about the way life takes different turns and how events shape our world, and how we as individuals create our own reality. Always remember that you are in the driver's seat: if you think you are not, then who is?

Black magic is the use of natural energy and the manipulation of these forces to gain control over others, and the use of this powerful energy to benefit only oneself. In black magic, there is only one tenet you need to keep in mind, and that is 'what ever you sow, so shall you reap'.

Earth magic involves using the energies of the earth, water, wind, fire, plant life, and mineral deposits in the form of stones. Out of all magic practices this is the easiest to do, as it involves very simple methods that draw upon the energies of your environment and the self, while harming none. Earth magic is what is described throughout this book and is sometimes used in combination with white magic.

RITUAL, SPELL, BLESSING AND CEREMONY

Rituals or rites are an important feature of all cultures, both past and present, because they help to maintain the integrity of a community or group and prepare each individual for the role they play in this life. Rituals are physical enactments of a spiritual journey into the self. A ritual is another word for spell and spell is also another word for blessing. Ceremony is closely related to all three nouns, and it is important that you choose to use the word you feel most comfortable with. I like to use all four words, depending on the context.

Unfortunately, many people have a negative outlook on spells and rituals and most of what is said about them is merely a distorted view of what is in reality a very natural way of life. Each of us has a ritual which we do everyday without even thinking about it. We may have a cup of tea or coffee first thing in the morning or we might visit the same restaurant every few weeks. A wedding is the most common ritual still practised by most cultures and I am sure you can think of hundreds more. These are only one way in which we have rituals in our lives. Imagine what would happen if you started doing spells or rituals to bring good luck into your life. Magic would improve your life a hundredfold. Give some thought to creating a little magic in your life. When you perform a ritual, spell, blessing or ceremony you are also honouring Mother Earth.

Ritual is about creating the seemingly impossible as possible, it is a formalised use of symbols that can be done with or without tools. Using such tools will help to keep your focus on the task at hand. Not only can magic bring about physical changes in your life, it can also effect increased self-esteem that will complement your daily life.

Use only tools and symbols that resound within you, ones that you feel connected to. These will work for better results. If you are a beginner in the art of magic, use the ingredients and instructions laid out in the following pages.

Spells will not guarantee you love or luck or your heart's desire, unless you are willing to look at the beliefs that prevent you from living your life to the fullest. These beliefs are like old patterns that you continue to follow, for example, giving up yourself in a relationship, not taking responsibility for your actions, or taking no action to change things that do not serve you. Spells or rituals cannot and will not work for you, if you are not willing to look at change.

'For things to change first must I.'

The words you use in a spell to accomplish a desired change should only be words that, when spoken, help you to feel as if you have aquired what you asked for. You may wish to change the words given in this book to suit yourself. This is perfectly correct, as long as you remember to only use positive words. Write or say the words in a way that serves your highest good and that of others.

Ceremony is derived from the Latin for 'sacredness'. It is an ancient way to make concrete what has been learned through active imagination and dreamwork. Ceremony affirms our relationship to a sacred time we have shared with our inner world. We create ceremony to enhance our lives and to gain more understanding of how we are one with the earth. Simple ceremonies are performed merely by spending time alone in nature to honour our source and creator.

To ensure the right environment for a ritual, spell, blessing or ceremony you need to follow a few guidelines to help create it. The following guidelines do just that so please follow these steps before performing any of the rituals given in this book. Please note: Even if is not stated in the spell or ritual, it is necessary to cast a circle around your magical work before beginning. SO MOTE IT BE

Important Steps to a Ritual

- ☑ ELIMINATE ANYTHING AND ANYONE THAT WILL INTERRUPT YOU OR INVADE YOUR PRIVACY, AND TAKE THE TELEPHONE OFF THE HOOK.

- ☑ HAVE ALL THE INGREDIENTS NEEDED BY YOUR SIDE SO THEY ARE EASY TO GET AT.

- ☑ TAKE A BATH USING THE BEST HERBS AND FLOWERS FOR YOUR WORK.

- ☑ WEAR ONLY NATURAL FIBRE CLOTHING AND NO JEWELLERY.

- ☑ TAKE AS MUCH TIME AS YOU NEED.

- ☑ CREATE A SACRED SPACE TO PERFORM ALL SPELLS, RITUALS, BLESSINGS AND CEREMONIES AS IT IS BEST TO HAVE ONLY ONE PLACE IN WHICH TO DO YOUR SPECIAL WORK.

- ☑ CLEAR A SPACE WITH THE USE OF INCENSE. THE SMOKE WILL REMOVE ANY NEGATIVE ENERGY. (NATIVE AMERICAN INDIANS USED A SMUDGE STICK MADE FROM SAGE, CEDAR OR SWEETGRASS. THE SMOKE WAS SAID TO CLEAR THE AIR AND PROTECT FROM EVIL.)

- ☑ CAST A CIRCLE AROUND YOUR SPACE.

Good Moon Times for Rituals and Spells

Traditionally, the moon has been used as a guide to the best time for performing rituals. It is not always important to follow the moon, as if you feel it is the right time to perform your spell, then listen to your inner wisdom or wait until the moon is in the right position to bring you your wishes.

The following movements are considered the best moon times. Use them as you need.

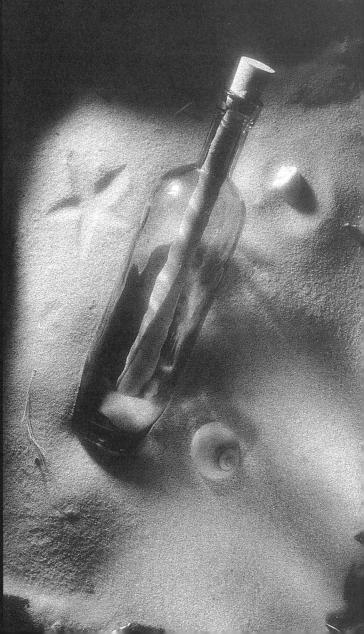

- ☑ FULL MOON — INDICATES STATUS QUO, COMPLETION AND ACHIEVEMENT.
- ☑ WAXING MOON — MEANS POWERFUL CHANGES SIGNIFYING WHOLENESS, CREATIVITY AND REGENERATION.
- ☑ WANING MOON — RESULTS IN BANISHING OLD WAYS AND OLD RELATIONSHIPS.
- ☑ NEW MOON — BRINGS ABOUT NEW BEGINNINGS, THE START OF NEW RELATIONSHIPS AND NEW JOBS.

CASTING A CIRCLE

Creating a Sacred Space

The reason we cast a circle before performing any magic is to provide a space where we can have directed energy for the creation of a magical need, and to protect us from being disturbed. This is done each time you wish to perform any spell, ritual, blessing or ceremony.

A circle offers protection to the person during ritual, mainly protection from unwanted influences. There is no one way to cast a circle.

For the beginner, please use the method shown here. For future reference, it is a good idea to read more books for other methods until you find one way that suits you best. This is the method that has suited my needs but each individual needs to find one of their own.

To cast a circle, follow these steps.

◪ LOCATE THE FOUR DIRECTIONS — EAST, SOUTH, WEST AND NORTH.

◪ IMAGINE THERE IS A PHYSICAL CIRCLE OR MAGICAL RING AROUND YOU AND THE SPACE YOU ARE OCCUPYING.

◪ CALL IN ALL FOUR DIRECTIONS, SAYING:

'I cast this magical space to create, may it protect me from unwanted energies and draw to me

◪ THEN IMAGINE THAT YOU HAVE A WHITE LIGHT AROUND YOU AND KNOW THAT THIS LIGHT CAN BE CALLED UPON WHENEVER YOU FEEL THE NEED TO HAVE PROTECTION.

ANOINTING OILS

Scented oils have been used for centuries, as throughout history people have been aware of the effects of scented plants and flowers on their minds, bodies and emotions. For the main part, in the beginning, scented oils were used to heal. They then became part of everyday life and began to be used in baths, to anoint sacred objects as part of ritual and ceremony, and to be offered to the gods and goddesses in the form of incense, such as frankincense. Frankincense, and incense generally, was found to heighten the senses for spiritual rites. Along with these uses, scented oils were also used for anointing the body. Cleopatra used a selection of oils to attract her many admirers. The wearing of scented oils was said to attract good fortune or love. This is where modern aromatherapy began and today has once again become part of our everyday lives.

The following blends have been created to employ the magical properties of these essential oils. This type of usage is an offshoot of aromatherapy, as oils are utilising the non-physical energy within our bodies. To introduce you to traditional aromatherapy I have included a few combinations that are used by practitioners of the art, for relaxation or inspiration, or even to freshen an environment. If you would like to know more about aromatherapy, there are many books available on the subject, a few of which are listed at the end of this book.

and in me only energy that works with light and love. All other energy begone.'

Aromatherapy, in its use of essential oils, will also give you a magical view to life, so enjoy the pleasure of the many fragrances and have fun creating your own special combinations. You may wish to make your own essential oils from fresh flowers but there are many companies around these days that make oils with great care and a good understanding of how to treat them. As you make your own magical blends, remember that pure oils are expensive, so choose your combinations with care. The following oils are only a guide to what may be made, feel free to make up your own blends as you become more familiar with the different oils and their associated properties.

Essential oils can be used for many purposes. They can help you to create a magical environment and their fragrant scent is useful as well. Use oils to dress the candles, as this will impregnate the candle with your own personal vibrations and charge it with your life force. You can also anoint a candle to increase the intention of the blessing or spell, or wear oils to attract love and luck, put oil in burners to scent the environment and dispel bad vibrations, or add a few drops of oil to your charms or to a bath, or even rub oil on objects, such as crystals or stones to increase their effectiveness and use. You be the judge of how best to utilise oils in your magic.

To make up your oil blends, you will need a selection of 30 ml (1 fl oz) bottles (found at your chemist), or use any small bottles that are clean (wash bottles out with pure alcohol) and that appeal to you. You will also need a selection of base oils (such as almond, avocado or apricot oil) and essential oils, a selection of dried herbs (such as mint and cinnamon), a 200 ml (6½ fl oz) mixing bottle, and an eye dropper for each oil.

While blending oils focus your intention on the property of the oil you are using, for example love or prosperity, etc. When you are blending become an alchemist and charge the oil not only with your intention, but with new life so that whatever you wish for in life will come to you. After adding the essential oils to the base oil — you should make your base oil up in advance keeping the same focus — swirl the bottle clockwise, then put the oil away for a few days, wrapped in a cloth, which may be coloured if you so desire, it is your ritual. Each day take the bottle out and swirl it in a clockwise direction saying.

'May the spirits of this oil help bring my highest good. So mote it be.'

Then thank the spirits of the herbs and oils, in your own words, using words that mean something to you.

The sacred act of anointing can be done everyday. You can anoint yourself and others by placing a drop of oil between the eyebrows and saying,

'My Blessing is for love and joy.'

Remember your intention while anointing.

Please note that essential oils can and do irritate the skin, so do not put them on the skin undiluted.

PROSPERITY OIL

Open your heart to have prosperity in your life.
You will need to gather:
8 drops of each of cinnamon, orange, and chamomile essential oils
2 drops ginger essential oil
30 ml (1 fl oz) almond oil
1 stick of cinnamon

Add the essential oils to the almond base oil and shake to mix well. Place the cinnamon stick in the bottle. Rub oil on your wallet or on candles for a prosperity spell, or on lottery tickets etc, to bring prosperity into your life.

LOVE OIL

Create a loving space.
You will need to gather:
6 drops of each of rose, lavender and coriander essential oils
30 ml (1 fl oz) avocado oil
½ a vanilla bean

Add the essential oils to the avocado base oil and shake well to mix. Place the vanilla bean in the bottle. Put oil on love letters (even your bills!), or add a few drops to a bath, or wear oil on a special date, send a bottle of oil to your lover, or place oil in an oil burner to create a loving environment. This oil is also good to use as a massage oil.

LUCK OIL

To draw luck.

You will need to gather:
6 drops of each of thyme, anise and mint essential oils
30 ml (1 fl oz) olive oil
1 sprig fresh mint

Add essential oils to the olive base oil and shake well to mix. Place the mint sprig in the bottle. Put a drop of oil on your pen before an exam, or add a few drops to a resume before sending it to a prospective employer.

FRIENDSHIP OIL

Helps to strengthen friendship.

You will need to gather:
4 drops honeysuckle essential oil
2 drops basil essential oil
2 drops spearmint essential oil
30 ml (1 fl oz) almond oil
1 sprig fresh spearmint

Add the essential oils to the base almond oil and shake well to mix. Place the spearmint sprig in the bottle. Put a few drops of oil in a card or letter to a friend.

HEALING EMOTIONS OIL

Clears space to allow healing.

You will need to gather:
7 drops sandalwood essential oil
3 drops violet fragrant oil
2 drops eucalyptus essential oil

30 ml (1 fl oz) grapeseed oil
1 small piece of sandalwood

Add essential oils to grapeseed base oil and shake well to mix. Place the piece of sandalwood in the bottle. Use this oil in an oil burner or rub a small amount on the heart and chest area as this will allow all your feelings to come to the surface so that they can be released.

PEACE AND HARMONY OIL

To restore balance to your environment.

You will need to gather:
3 drops jasmine essential oil
5 drops lilac essential oil
2 drops magnolia essential oil
30 ml (1 fl oz) sunflower oil

Add essential oils to sunflower base oil and shake well to mix. Use oil in an oil burner or anoint a white candle with the oil and dedicate the candle to harmony.

OTHER OILS

Please note that the scent of some blends may be very subtle so do not add more essential oil for a stronger scent, as the blends are already magical and effective.

Essential Oils and Their Properties

The following list is based on traditional aromatherapy usage and guidelines.

PSYCHIC AWARENESS
BAY LEAVES, CINNAMON, NUTMEG, MUGWORT, LEMONGRASS, AND STAR ANISE

MEDITATION
CHAMOMILE, FRANKINCENSE, AND SANDALWOOD

STRESS
BASIL, ROSE, AND LAVENDER

DEPRESSION
CLARY SAGE, ROSE, AND YLANG-YLANG

SPIRITUALITY
CEDAR, MYRRH, AND SANDALWOOD

DREAMS
CLARY SAGE, MUGWORT, JASMINE, AND CALENDULA

To blend oils for the above purposes (see page 21), blend essential oils in a base oil of apricot or avocado oil. Add a few drops of each oil to a bottle and shake well to mix. Oils can be used in an oil burner, or mixed with herbs to make a pillow. For example juniper berries can be scented with the Dream oil and put in a cotton or silk square and be sewn up as an eye pillow. Cut out the material in an eye shape to fit over your eyes and sew a ribbon to each end, long enough to tie around your head. Remember to let the oil settle for a few days so that it will not irritate your eyes.

COLOUR MAGIC

Using Candles, Crystals and Oils

Colour was used by the ancient Egyptians in their temples for healing. In India, colour is associated with the chakras, which are the energy centres of the body. Many other ancient cultures also associated colour with energy, as colour effects our moods and feelings. Even today we talk of being green with envy, or feeling blue, and different colours can be used in healing the body and in meditation to stabilise these emotions and harmonise the body and spirit.

Colour magic uses the essence within a colour and its vibrations, as every colour has its own unique vibration. When used together, the essence and vibration of a colour form a magical ritual that will enhance the energies. It is powerful magic, yet safe. Using colour is fun and can help to create a more magical ritual. All it takes is for you to look inside yourself and ask for inner guidance as to which colour best suits the occasion. Colour stimulates the power within, as it is the flowering of one's potential, and represents living in harmony with the laws of nature. Along with colour, the use of candles and oils also aid in enhancing the overall effect of the magical ritual, particularly since lighting candles represents the time to usher in the illumination of the soul to celebrate rebirth.

When deciding on the colour of the candle choose the oil to match, as these candle rituals are designed to be done when you do not have a major wish. These mini-rituals can be performed every day if you prefer, as they will help you to remember to live a magical life. If you like, use more than one candle, as sometimes a few different colours used together are more effective. I have used 10 to 20 candles on many occasions in order to perform a ritual or ceremony.

Before lighting a candle contemplate your dedication, depending on the colour of the candle, and then take a sharp object and carve the desired symbol onto the candle. To enhance the candle magic, use the corresponding crystal from the list below (see pages 24–25). If you would like to use the crystal with the candle, hold the crystal in your non-writing hand and charge it with your life force. Then place the crystal in front of the candle.

Once this is completed, take a few minutes to clear your mind and be ready to visualise what it is that you need. Then light the candle saying to yourself:

'I dedicate this candle to love and abundance', or, *'May my wish be taken up in the light'*.

Keep the crystal with you or use it in your meditations, knowing that the crystal is already charged with your intention. You may want to anoint the crystals with oil.

Always snuff your candles out rather than blowing them, as this will keep the magic in the candle and you can relight it in the future with the same intention. Anointing candles adds to the magic, so add a few drops to your fingertips while visualising your need and then rub the oil into the candle. The scent will carry in the air when the candle is lit, reminding you once again of your wish.

CANDLE, CRYSTAL AND OIL COLOUR COMBINATIONS

1. WHITE

CANDLE: White — for peace and spirituality
CRYSTAL: Clear Quartz — for balance and to bring about peacefulness and spirituality
OIL: Anoint with jasmine or lily essential oil
BLESSING: 'I dedicate this candle to the peace essential to my spiritual nourishment.'
AND SO IT IS

2. RED

CANDLE: Red — for passion, love and compassion
CRYSTAL: Rose Quartz — to aid in the development of self love and compassion
OIL: Anoint with rose essential oil
BLESSING: 'May my wish of a passionate, loving life be taken up in the light of this candle.'
SO MOTE IT BE

3. YELLOW

CANDLE: Yellow — for joy and friendship
CRYSTAL: Citrine — to bring about cheerfulness, hope and light heartedness
OIL: Anoint with bergamot essential oil
BLESSING: 'I dedicate this candle to emotional balance in all my friendships.'
AND SO SHALL IT BE

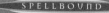

4. GREEN

CANDLE: Green — for abundance, luck and harmony
CRYSTAL: Jade — for abundance, prosperity, and luck
OIL: Anoint with lemon oil
BLESSING: 'May my wish to open to universal support be taken up in
the light of this candle'.
ALL IS ONE

5. BLUE

CANDLE: Blue — for healing and protection
CRYSTAL: Sodalite — to help maintain clarity, truth and creative
expression
OIL: Anoint with sage oil
BLESSING: 'I dedicate this candle to the healing rays of the angels.'
AND SO SHALL IT BE

6. PURPLE

CANDLE: Purple — for spiritual and material wealth
CRYSTAL: Amethyst — for calming, healing and protection
OIL: Anoint with cinnamon oil
BLESSING: 'May my wish to allow my needs to be met be taken up
in the light of this candle.'
ALL IS ONE

Crystal Magic

Crystals have been used in magic for eons and each one has its own unique qualities and healing abilities. Crystals amplify the energy that is around them, and, when used in a magical ritual, they can amplify the intentions of the energy that is focused on them. Crystals will also help remove unwanted energies, so increase your thought power by using them in rituals and spells.

Collect crystals and make them yours by doing the following ritual. Wash each crystal using either sea salt or rock salt, then leave the crystal in the salted water overnight. Look at the crystal and imagine a white light covering it. Know that all the unwanted energies are removed. Now hold the crystal in your hands and feel the energy emanating from it, then focus your intention into the crystal. Do this for as long as you need, and say an affirmation if you wish. You may want to write a special affirmation to say for each of your crystals. Crystals used for your meditations should have a special bag where they are kept after use. If you like to have your crystals around the home or office make sure you cleanse them from time to time as they can pick up on negative energy. You are the best judge of this occurring, but it is more likely to happen if people pick them up and hold them. Some people do not mind others touching their crystals but that is a matter of personal choice. I personally keep the ones I do not want to be touched in and around my bedroom so they will only be charged with my energy.

Crystals are a thing of beauty and you may just like to have them around you because you like the look of them. You do not have to do anything special to them, as merely keeping them around your home or office creates beauty in your environment.

The following is a list of some of the many crystals and their magical properties. Use this list to choose appropriate crystals for your own personal rituals.

AGATE: FOR WORLDLY SUCCESS AND HAPPINESS

AMETHYST: COMBATS ADDICTION, SOOTHES STRESS, DRAWS HAPPINESS AND STRENGTHENS COMMITMENT

AVENTURINE: STIMULATES CREATIVITY

BLOOD STONE: HAS HEALING AND MAGICAL POWERS FOR CLEARING ENERGY

CITRINE: FOR ORGANISATION AND SELF ORDER, HELP WITH NIGHTMARES, OR FOR ABUNDANCE

CLEAR QUARTZ: FOR CLARITY, COURAGE, PROTECTION, AND PEACEFUL SLEEP

FLUORITE: A CATALYST STONE FOR SPIRITUAL GROWTH, AND DREAM STONE

HEMATITE: A GROUNDING STONE TO DRAW ILLNESS AWAY FROM BODY

JADE: A CONTEMPLATIVE STONE FOR ABUNDANCE, HEALING, AND PROSPERITY

LAPIS LAZULI: FOR UNSELFISH LOVE AND COMPASSION, SUCCESS AND TALENT

MOONSTONE: FOR NURTURING, INSPIRES TENDER LOVE

PEARL: LINKED WITH HIDDEN KNOWLEDGE AND PATIENCE

RED JASPER: A PROTECTIVE STONE FOR HEALING BELIEFS ABOUT BEAUTY

ROSE QUARTZ: FOR LOVE, FRIENDSHIP AND COMPASSION FOR SELF AND OTHERS

SODALITE: FOR PROTECTION

TURQUOISE: FOR PROTECTION

The Sacred Chamber Dream Diary N

CHARGING CRYSTALS

The following is a list of the best days to charge crystals with your intention, to use them in combination with the candles and scented oils to perform mini-rituals for specific purposes. Choose to charge the crystal on the day that best suits your intention.

MONDAY

PLANET: Moon — to heighten the intuition of one's inner self

CANDLE: White

CRYSTAL: Moonstone

OIL: Lavender essential oil

RITUAL: Place the crystal in front of the candle making a small altar. Anoint the candle with the oil and light it, calling on the goddess of intuition for help to balance the female energy.

TUESDAY

PLANET: Mars — for strength in goal-setting and motivation

CANDLE: Green

CRYSTAL: Red jasper

OIL: Pine essential oil

RITUAL: Place crystal in front of candle. Anoint the crystal with the oil and light the candle. Use this ritual when you are in need of courage and meditate on the candle.

WEDNESDAY

PLANET: Mercury — aids in communication and increases study skills

CANDLE: Purple

CRYSTAL: Citrine

OIL: Lemon essential oil

RITUAL: Place crystal in front of candle. Anoint candle with oil and light it. Have this crystal in your pocket when dealing with people or when studying.

THURSDAY

PLANET: Jupiter — to focus you on wealth, success and luck in your future

CANDLE: Green

CRYSTAL: Jade

OIL: Nutmeg essential oil

RITUAL: Anoint crystal with oil. Place crystal in front of candle and light the candle. Use this ritual when you need to create material wealth. Keep the crystal in a visible place.

FRIDAY

PLANET: Venus — for guidance given on romance and love

CANDLE: Pink

CRYSTAL: Rose quartz

OIL: Rose essential oil

RITUAL: Anoint the crystal with the oil. Place the crystal in front of the candle and light the candle. Dedicate the crystal to giving yourself and others compassion in dealing with all relationships.

PLANET: Saturn — to gain balance and patience through inner wisdom

CANDLE: Blue

CRYSTAL: Sodalite

OIL: Patchouli essential oil

RITUAL: Place crystal in front of candle. Place oil in an oil burner and use candle to light it. Burn oil before sleeping as it helps you to ask for inner wisdom.

SUNDAY

PLANET: Sun — helps to radiate joy and peace

CANDLE: Yellow

CRYSTAL: Tiger's eye

OIL: Cedar essential oil

RITUAL: Anoint crystal with the oil and place in front of candle. Light the candle and dedicate it to joy and peace. Give a few tiger's eye crystals away to friends and strangers to spread joy and peace.

Create your own ways of dedicating your crystals using your own intentions and affirmations so that the ritual will have special meaning for you. The above-mentioned dedications are only a few of the infinite possibilities open to you if you use your imagination.

The purpose of this ritual is to provide a special space for a couple to communicate their feelings and to work through any problems or upsets which may have occurred in their relationship.

Set up a regular time when you want to be in close and honest communication with your intimate partner. Alternatively, if you have a great urge to get something out into the open immediately, set aside a time which fits in with both of you at the next available opportunity.

Take the phone off the hook or unplug it. Create a safe, magical space which you can use for this ritual. A special rug on the floor could be all you may have. This is fine.

You will need to gather:
a special rug
cushions
crystals of your choice (see list page 27)
incense of your choice
drink such as wine, champagne or fruit juice
food such as fruit or other titbits to share or feed to each other
1 sacred candle (both people should choose the colour together according to the list on pages 24-25),
placed in a special candle holder
any other decorations of your choice such as flowers or plants

Have some relaxing music playing quietly in the background. Set up your space as you wish.

In this ritual, the couple should sit facing each other, with the candle burning in between them. Whoever wishes to start should reach for the candle, while contemplating what it is they want to say. The other person need only listen, as when they have the candle they will be able to speak whatever is true for them in reply. It is important to remember that there are always two sides to a problem.

The person holding the candle then addresses themselves to the candle, telling the candle what the situation is, how they feel about it or their partner and anything else they wish to communicate. Each person should speak from a place of truth, honesty and love inside themselves.

This is a very potent ritual to affirm one's deep feelings for a partner as well as a place to clear any upsets or unspoken words. Feelings are communicated as if to a third person with the partner merely listening. In this way, any problems in the relationship are taken outside the couple and become a shared situation which both can work on from a different perspective, without any feelings of blame, shame or denial. When the first speaker has completed what they want to say, they move the candle back into the middle. The other person then reaches for the candle and proceeds to communicate with it while their partner listens in the same manner as before. This ritual can be used in combination with other spells or rituals.

MAGICAL POUCHES

Magical pouches, cachés and charms have been used in most magical work for many years, as they are usually the easiest form of earth magic. Known as wanga, gris-gris, mojo bags and putsi-pockets, these pouches or bags are found all around the world, in such cultures as the Australian Aboriginals, the American Indians, African Voodoo societies and most European cultures. All these cultures employ pouches stuffed with various empowering ingredients, that they believe to bring health, luck, or protection, etc. The pouches or bags were worn either by the maker or were given to others to wear or to place somewhere easily visible.

These pouches can contain any number of things, the following list of items (see page 36) will help you to choose the right ones to use for your purpose. Some cultures have used animal bones but I have not suggested the use of this type of item.

The colour of the pouch helps to heighten the energies you are working with. The following colours (see page 35) are to be used only as a guide. If in doubt, rely on your inner guidance: if it tells you that the colour I have suggested does not feel right, do not worry as your own choice will always be perfect.

Charms to wear for protection can be almost anything, such as a bag, a stone, a feather or all of these things combined. The most common charm is the pouch which combines a few items. This pouch can be shaped like a bag, or a heart, or any shape that represents your purpose.

A simple bag could be made from a piece of material cut in a square big enough to put a few items in, perhaps a square 15 cm (6 in) by 15 cm (6 in), but the size of the pouch is your own personal choice. Sew the edges and decorate it to please yourself. Before deciding on the shape, mix all the ingredients you intend to use together, and keep the focus of your intention on love, luck or whatever else you desire. Then tie the pouch with string or ribbon very tightly so that the contents will not fall out, but make sure you can untie the pouch because you may want to refresh it with more of the appropriate oil.

To make the pouch yours, sit quietly and experience what it feels like to have what you asked for, visualise what your wish looks like and know that you will receive what you need. Then hold the pouch in your hands and smell it, while visualising what your wish looks like. Do this everyday or as many times as you need to, and every time you see it, it will remind you of your wish.

Make only one pouch at a time as you need to have only one focus otherwise you will not be able to keep that particular intention clear. Magic happens only when you expend total energy on one intention. Keep in mind that you have to think about what you want and need as you can have anything you put your focus on. Remember: be careful what you ask for.

COLOURS FOR MAGICAL POUCHES

The following is a list of colours of materials to be used to make a magical pouch. The material for the pouch should be a natural product such as silk or leather, or any natural fibre.

BLACK: Absorption of negativity, destruction of negativity, and rebirth of spirit

BLUE: Protection, healing, patience, sleep, and compassion

BROWN: Healing for animals and homes

GREEN: Luck, fertility, healing, growth, employment, and cooperation

ORANGE: Legal matters, success, attraction, and kindness

PINK: Emotional love and overcoming anger

PURPLE: Wealth, power, psychic powers, and strengthens willpower

RED: Passion, sensual love, strength, courage, enthusiasm, promotes good health and life force

WHITE: Peace, truth, halting gossip, purity, and breaks curses

YELLOW: Friendship, wisdom, happiness, joy, instils confidence and humility

If there is any colour not listed that you wish to use, and you do not know the magical meaning behind the colour, instil the colour with whatever meaning you wish it to have. This is very powerful magic because you are using your own intuition to create magic. That is how magic began, with one person gaining a result from the colours they used.

DAYS FOR MAKING MAGICAL POUCHES

Making a magical pouch on a particular day will add to the focus of the pouch and your intention.

SUNDAY: Represented by the SUN — fortune, new beginnings, hope

MONDAY: Represented by the MOON — dreams

TUESDAY: Represented by MARS — matrimony

WEDNESDAY: Represented by MERCURY — communication

THURSDAY: Represented by JUPITER — joy, riches, wealth

FRIDAY: Represented by VENUS — love, friendships

SATURDAY: Represented by SATURN — life building, protection

Herbs, oils and plants that can be used in your Magical Caché or Pouch

The following ingredients can be utilised as the dried herb or plant or the essential oil of the plant or herb. Each is linked to a particular purpose, so choose from the list below those that best suit your needs.

HEALTH: THYME, PEPPERMINT, HOPS, EUCALYPTUS, DANDELION, PUMPKIN SEEDS, FEVERFEW, MANDRAKE ROOT, LEMON, PINE, SPEARMINT AND BAY LEAVES.

LOVE: BASIL, YARROW, ORRISROOT, MYRTLE, ROSEMARY, THYME, GINGER AND CHAMOMILE. (SEE OTHER ELEMENTS IN LOVE CHARMS, PAGE 57.)

LUCK: ALFALFA SEEDS, BASIL, MUSTARD SEEDS, GINGER, ROSEMARY, LEMON, ANISE, HOLLY AND CORN.

MONEY: CLOVER, NUTMEG, THYME, ECHENACEA, COLTSFOOT, ALLSPICE, ALMOND, BERGAMOT, JASMINE, CINNAMON, DILL, ELDER FLOWER, GINGER, IRISH MOSS AND NUTMEG.

PROTECTION: GARLIC, BASIL, BAY LEAVES, FRANKINCENSE, St JOHN'S WORT, GRAPEVINE, CARAWAY SEEDS, SAGE, ROSEMARY, IRON, SANDALWOOD, HEATHER, PINE, IVY, MANDRAKE ROOT, JUNIPER BERRIES, SUNFLOWER SEEDS AND ONION.

PURIFICATION: PEPPERMINT SAGE, CEDAR, SWEET GRASS, LAVENDER, LEMON AND LIME.

SUCCESS: CINNAMON, IRISH MOSS, VERVAIN LEAVES, POPPY SEEDS AND HONEYSUCKLE.

SYMBOLS

Symbols can be used to add a new energy to your charm or magical pouch. The following are a small selection of the most common ones used in magic.

You are free to decide the meaning of the symbols you use, as their meaning only needs to hold significance for the individual using them. You could start a scrapbook with your symbols and your own corresponding meanings for them. The secret of the symbol is revealed to those who work with them.

Each symbol needs to be brought to life in some way. For example, these symbols can be drawn on paper, or you can make them yourself out of clay. Use your imagination to find a way to represent the symbol you want to use. Another way to bring symbols to life is to look through old magazines and find pictures of the various symbols, then use these pictures to make a treasure map on card or paper of the things you desire. Hang it on the wall where you will see it everyday. This treasure map will remind you of your wishes and keep your focus on them. These symbols can be put into pouches, and worn by you to bring the energy of the symbol to you.

ACORN: TRUE LOVE

ANCHOR: SALVATION AND HOPE

BEE: SUCCESS IN BUSINESS

BOOK: WISDOM

BUTTERFLY: TRANSFORMATION AND FREEDOM

CANDLES: THE SEEKING OF LIGHT TO DISPEL THE DARKNESS

COINS: RICHES, LUCK AND MONEY

CORN DOLL: FERTILITY, FOR WOMEN WISHING FOR PREGNANCY

CROSS: FAITH IN AN IDEA

DICE: LUCK OR MONEY

DRAGON: STRENGTH, SELF-DISCIPLINE, JOY, GOOD HEALTH, FERTILITY AND TO WARD OFF EVIL

FOUR LEAF CLOVER: LUCK

HEART: THE CONNECTION TO LOVE WHICH BRINGS WITH IT HARMONY IN OUR LIFE, PLEASURE AND COMPASSION

HONEY: FERTILITY AND ABUNDANCE

KEY: PROSPERITY

MERMAID: IDEALISED AND ELUSIVE FEMININE BEAUTY

MUSHROOM: HAPPINESS AND FERTILITY

OLIVE BRANCH: PEACE OFFERING

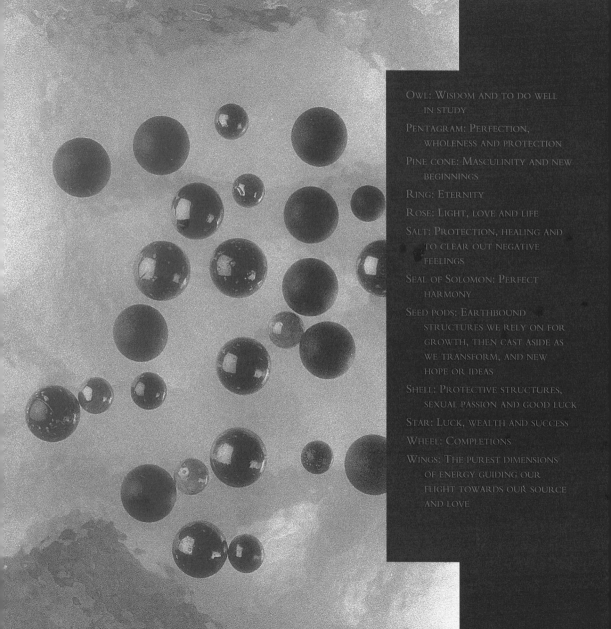

OWL: WISDOM AND TO DO WELL
IN STUDY

PENTAGRAM: PERFECTION,
WHOLENESS AND PROTECTION

PINE CONE: MASCULINITY AND NEW
BEGINNINGS

RING: ETERNITY

ROSE: LIGHT, LOVE AND LIFE

SALT: PROTECTION, HEALING AND
TO CLEAR OUT NEGATIVE
FEELINGS

SEAL OF SOLOMON: PERFECT
HARMONY

SEED PODS: EARTHBOUND
STRUCTURES WE RELY ON FOR
GROWTH, THEN CAST ASIDE AS
WE TRANSFORM, AND NEW
HOPE OR IDEAS

SHELL: PROTECTIVE STRUCTURES,
SEXUAL PASSION AND GOOD LUCK

STAR: LUCK, WEALTH AND SUCCESS

WHEEL: COMPLETIONS

WINGS: THE PUREST DIMENSIONS
OF ENERGY GUIDING OUR
FLIGHT TOWARDS OUR SOURCE
AND LOVE

Feathers are symbolic of the great spirit. Each colour has its own meaning:

BLUE: PEACE, HEALING AND FOR LOVE TO ENLIVEN YOUR DAYS

GREEN: MONEY, GROWTH AND AN ADVENTURESOME LOVER

RED: COURAGE AND GOOD FORTUNE

WHITE: PURIFICATION, HOPE AND TO SEE THE TRUTH ABOUT YOUR LOVER

YELLOW: INTELLIGENCE, BLESSING AND TO BEWARE OF AN UNTRUE LOVER

Runes:

 HEALTH

 LEGAL MATTERS

 LOVE

 LUCK

 PROTECTION

 WEALTH AND TO INCREASE FINANCES

THE HEAVENS STONE SET

Divination is the magical act of discovering the unknown by interpreting random patterns or symbols. This section will show you how to make your own divination tool.

Collect pieces of ocean-tumbled glass. Ocean beach is the best place to collect good pieces. Make sure that the pieces you choose are of a similar size. If you cannot find glass pieces, you can also use the clay from craft shops or pieces of wood.

Next, buy some craft paint in your favourite colour. I personally use gold, but it is up to you what colour you choose. Paint symbols that represent the planets on each piece of glass or other material. You will find the symbols I use next to each planet in the list below (see page 41).

Make up a book for your symbols and their explanations. You may want to use recycled paper or handmade paper for the pages of your book. Write in the explanations listed below (see page 41) in your book and draw the corresponding symbol beside it. The words I have used are guidelines only and you are the one that needs to interpret them. The best way to use the divination stones is to hold a question in your mind and then pull out a stone and read the appropriate explanation for it.

To store your stones you can either put them into a bag (one you make yourself is best), or wrap them in a piece of material (silk is the most appropriate). You can also use the cloth to put them on while you are reading the stones. Once you have worked with them for a while you may want to do a reading for your friends and family. Follow your intuition as to the meaning of each stone, as this makes for the best readings and the greatest accuracy.

☉ The Sun

Signifies assertiveness in a situation, will, ability to take action, or to use charisma to gain insights.

☽ The Moon

Signifies emotions, travel, reconciliations, the ability to nurture a loved one, or to use female energy to gain insights, to write down dreams, or to have time alone.

☿ Mercury

Signifies communication, the arts, the need to clear up a broken agreement, or travel, analysis of self and playfulness.

♀ Venus

Signifies the extent of love, peace and harmony. Practice holding yourself with grace, charm, kindness, acceptance and diplomacy.

♄ Saturn

Signifies discipline, structure, sleep, the need to be humble, the desire for purification of the home, or solitude and challenges.

♂ Mars

Signifies dynamic energy, courage, and success. Use your current drive constructively and take action.

♃ Jupiter

Signifies humour, riches, meditation, and physical health. Your passions will show you the way to your next opportunity. Buy a lottery ticket.

♅ Uranus

Signifies change, insights and awareness. Ask your intuition what needs to change? Capitalise on your creative impulses.

♆ Neptune

Signifies subconscious, secrets, hidden things, the ability to clarify the issue and sensitivity.

♇ Pluto

Signifies the need to be easy on yourself as this is the planet of major transformations, rebirth and creation. Use your intuition here.

Sacred Chamber Dream Diary Natures Life Force Cast

CHAPTER ONE LOVE — LOVE IS WITHIN

'Love is the answer.'

Love itself is a form of magic that transforms and excites not just the lovers themselves but also those around them. Magic can bring about changes in the twinkle of a eye but it is no substitute for real personal growth and transformation. These latter are required to make a loving relationship prosper, as only a person who is truly committed can make a relationship last.

Love is often misunderstood and we sometimes feel that it is something outside ourselves. If we feel this way we will never be truly happy, as true love is within us and if we do not look inside ourselves, we will never find it. The feeling we have when we are attracted to someone is so overwhelming: it is what makes us think we will do 'anything for love'. This feeling is wonderful, but problems arise when we think we get love only from this other person we are attracted to, and we then only feel good around that person. In thinking this, we cut ourselves off from the energy called universal love which is found within. At this point we start to manipulate or control other people and situations, and we find ourselves left with anything but love.

When performing love rituals keep firmly in your mind that you are doing it for yourself and to connect with the love within you. While performing the spells and making your charms, be sure to have fun, as lightness of heart is very important to enjoying the moment and having the right energy to bring a new life into being. The following rituals are for those who desire a life that is full of love.

THE MIRROR OF VENUS
The Mirror of Love —Finding the Love Within

The essence of this ritual is to feel the magic of the love within you flowing out and giving you a new lease on life.

These rituals are for those who truly want to experience love, everyday in every way, and wish to connect with their inner partner. This is our first true step to self love. Each of us have male and female sides to our beings, and we need to come to terms with these aspects of ourselves and stop projecting these traits onto potential partners. The better we feel about ourselves, the better a partner we will be to someone else. It may sound strange but when you really think of it, if we prevent ourselves from having our heart's desire, how can we have a loving relationship? We need to work at loving the person we are without judgements, and to start accepting what we are, what we look like, etc. For this to happen, we need only look at our limited beliefs, as these beliefs could be the reason why we do not have the love of ourselves or of a partner.

The first step of this ritual is to look around your life and see the things you wish to change and/or want to improve upon. These could be physical, material or spiritual, depending on your need and desire for change. Then, set up a mirror so that you can sit before it and see yourself. Ask yourself questions about who you are now, and how you treat yourself.

HERE ARE SOME QUESTIONS YOU MAY WANT TO ASK:

1. DO I TAKE TIME AND CARE TO NURTURE MYSELF AND MY BODY?

2. DO I FEEL COMFORTABLE IN MY BODY AND MY ENVIRONMENT?

3. DO I GIVE MYSELF SPECIAL TREATS?

4. IS MY LIFE FLOWING WITH ENERGY?

5. ARE THINGS AND PEOPLE GETTING ME DOWN?

Listen to your response — you should be allowing your inner beauty to shine through. Think about how you would change some of your beliefs which prevent you from having all your needs met. You need to open your heart and let the love within you come forth. Follow the next steps (see pages 45–49) to help you gain a new way of nurturing yourself.

LOVE WEEK

Keep a journal of your love week to write down the insights you gain by doing the following exercises. This week is for you alone. It should be fun and full of love, but the only one that will determine how it will be is you. Make a stand to take some responsibility for how your life is, and to positively change it for the better.

DAY ONE

Rise before dawn, walk to a nearby sanctuary (any special and peaceful place will do), and re-experience the wonder of the day's rebirth. Find a place where you can sit down and think about how wonderful life is. Keep thinking beautiful thoughts — when a negative thought comes in just ask it to leave. Imagine yourself in a time or place when you felt good. It may even be where you are now. Visualise, smell and feel that environment, experience what it feels like to be a tree, the sky or anything else you see. Know that you are protected in whatever you do.

Now is the time for you to write an affirmation to start the week with, such as 'My life is filled with love, joy and happiness'. Your own words are the most powerful so sit and feel whatever is right for you. Keep your affirmation with you throughout the week, and look at it daily. You may like to write it on a card and place it where you will see it each morning.

Try to visit the ocean, so that you can absorb the splendour of the rising or setting sun. Realise that no matter what your flaws and challenges may be, you are a light to the world.

DAY TWO

First thing in the morning, relax with a cup of the following brew:

Take a handful of chamomile flowers (these are good for soothing your spirit) and a handful of jasmine tea (to connect with your spirit). Bring 500 ml (16 fl oz) spring or filtered water to the boil and steep flowers and tea in the water. Sweeten to taste with honey, sugar or lemon juice. While brewing tea, visualise yourself being filled with white light so that you are fully connected with your body. Think loving thoughts about how your body is supported and how your body is your strength. While sipping this healing brew imagine it filling you with clear insight for the day ahead, and allow love to shine through you.

DAY THREE

Send flowers to yourself (yes you are worth it) or better still visit a garden where you can pick your own flowers.

DAY FOUR

Find a yoga centre and start yoga, as it is an excellent way of connecting with your spirit.

or

Write on handmade paper affirmations such as 'I love my body' and 'I love you', and put them up all over your home, for example on the mirror in the bathroom or in the bedroom. Do not let what other people will think worry you. Each time you feel someone is judging you, or you are judging yourself, say to yourself this affirmation:

'What other people think of me is none of my concern, only what I think of myself concerns me.'

What you say to yourself is what manifests itself in your life as your attitude: either good, or bad, or indifferent. What you say thus becomes very powerful magic.

DAY FIVE

Make yourself a pomander love charm. A good day to make this charm is a Friday, as this is the day that Venus, the planet of love, rules the heavens.

You will need to gather:
1 medium to large orange
500 g (16 oz) whole cloves
1 tablespoon ground ginger
1 tablespoon ground cinnamon
1 tablespoon ground orrisroot
6 red candles
½ tablespoon salt

Hold the orange in your hands, visualising the love within, and keep this focus as you put the cloves into the orange. Make your own designs in the pomander, arranging the cloves as you wish. Combine the three spices in a small bowl and roll the orange in the spices until it is completely covered, all the while keeping your focus on love. Leave the orange in the bowl for a few days, every so often rolling it around. When you feel it is ready to take out, place the orange in the middle of the 6 red candles, with which you have formed a circle (if you want to you can anoint your candles with love oil [see page 19]), and sprinkle the salt around the base of each candle. Light the candles, visualising love in your life, and let the candles burn out. The charm is now ready to use. If you want to hang the pomander, tie a red cord around the orange and hang it where you will see it every day, to remind you of the love that is around your life.

DAY SIX

Pamper yourself: visit a beauty therapist or give yourself a facial.

To give yourself a facial follow these steps:

Step 1: Cleanse your skin with sorbolene cream and water (or any natural base cream) to which you add the following oils —

2 drops geranium essential oil, for love
1 drop sweet orange essential oil, for uplifting spirits
1 drop lemon essential oil, for healing the spirit

As you cleanse your face, visualise your skin feeling alive and imagine that you are cleaning away the old way you have viewed yourself.

Step 2: Massage your skin very gently with a facial scrub. If you can, use one that has cinnamon essential oil, for wealth of spirit, and apricot kernels, for love, as its ingredients. The scrub will exfoliate the surface and leave your skin clean. When rinsing off the scrub, visualise new life coming forth.

Step 3: Apply a cleansing mask, with the following herbs and oils added to it. You may want to use a gauze so that it will be easier to wash off the mask. If so, place herbs over gauze, making sure you have cut out holes for your nose and mouth.

You will need to gather:
1 cup (60 g/2 oz) lavender flowers, to bring out the inner beauty
1 tablespoon dried rosemary, ground to a fine powder, for purification
2 drops rose essential oil, for love
1 drop eucalyptus essential oil, for healing

Mix all ingredients with a cream mask, and smooth onto skin, or over gauze. Leave on for 15 minutes, and relax and let your mind wander. Use this time to keep silent and allow the loving herbs to soothe your spirit.

Step 4: Wash off mask, pat skin dry with a soft towel, and then apply a skin toner which is appropriate to your skin type. A toner based on natural ingredients is better for the skin and spirit.

Step 5: Now for a gentle massage use a moisturising cream made from natural ingredients. Buy one for your skin type from a natural skin care company. As you massage, visualise how beautiful you are, not just on the outside but from within. If you continue to perform this ritual, you will be quite surprised at the change you will experience in how you feel about yourself and in how others see you.

Note: Always use skin care that does not harm any fluffy animals.

On the seventh day the lord did say to rest!

Rest, sleep in, spend the whole day in bed if you can. You may want to plan for this day so that you can make up a basket of goodies to keep with you, or else ask a friend to get the things you need. Asking may be your biggest challenge.

or

Spend sometime alone. Go on a picnic, lay on the beach, spend time relaxing in front of the heater or open fire, or go away by yourself and enjoy your own company.

When the week is over, relive everything that has happened and think of other ways to bring love into your life. This *Love Week* can be repeated many times, and I do encourage you to do it at least once a month, or choose one day each week to perform some part of it.

Lovers' Ritual

Preparing for a date with love and passion is as good as the ritual of the date itself, because you are able to create and then explore the most special place between two people. This alone brings about a wonderful magic feeling.

You will need to gather:
2 red candles
love oil (see page 19)
strawberries, or other food you both enjoy, in bite-size pieces
love potion (see pages 51-52)
willingness to express your love openly and truthfully

Make a time for this ritual when you will not be disturbed. Light the candles and say to each other:

'May our love and passion fill this space we now create.'

Run a bath for both of you and add a few drops of love oil to the water. Bathe each other and as you do so, say loving words to each other to wash away any negative feelings or worry. Have the food beside the bath and feed pieces of it to each other. Look into your partner's eyes and remember the first time you were together, re-experience the feelings of that time, and remember how wonderful it was.

Spend as much time as you need to in the bath and then dry each other and find a space to massage each other. It could be just the feet or it could be a whole body massage, it is up to the two of you to decide together. Use the love oil to massage each other with, and, while doing this, send loving feelings to your partner, giving all of yourself to them, for as long as the massage lasts.

One of the most important aspects of a loving union is the art of touch, so do not hesitate

to ask for the touch that you need. Take time out in your busy day to touch your partner to create an intimate connection with them. It may not sound magical but to create a great relationship sometimes it is the little things that are the most magical, and the smallest touch will make you feel enchanted and bewitched.

You may not want to have a bath or to massage the whole body, so just washing and massaging each other's feet is fine as long as you still create the intimate space. Prepare everything you need before you begin.

You will need to gather:
a bucket of warm water
love oil (see page 19)
fluffy towel to dry feet

Place a few drops of love oil in warm water. The bucket should be large enough to fit both feet in comfortably. Wash your partner's feet and pat them dry gently with the towel. Massage each foot with the love oil. As you massage each other, make sure you both have a turn. Many women feel they should give to their partners and not allow their partner to do things for them. Asking is very important: you should never forget to ask for your needs to be met, because you are special too.

When you have finished the massage share this love potion together:

LOVE PHILTRE

You will need to gather:
½ teaspoon dried lavender, ground
½ vanilla pod
2 cloves
1 stick cinnamon
boiling water
500 ml (16 fl oz) red wine

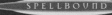

Blend together lavender, vanilla, cloves and cinnamon in a container and cover with boiling water. Allow to stand for 15 minutes then strain and add to red wine. Serve warm or cold.

As you drink the wine say these words together:

'May our love blossom and may we always speak to each other from the heart with love and respect.'

ALL IS ONE

ARROWS OF LOVE

Use the arrows of words to strike at the core of problems in your relationship. If you have trouble expressing your feelings, put your love in writing, as it provides you with an opportunity to express yourself and to say you are sorry, or to tell your partner of your anger. Verbal communication is great but the written word adds an extra touch that says you really care, and it also gives you the space to say what is on your mind. When feelings are written they can be put in such a way that there is no blame laid or judgement made. Feelings are intangibles that can not be changed and should not be lied about: they are simply the way they are and you cannot change other people only yourself.

'For things to change first I need to change.'

When problems are occurring in your relationships with others, take responsibility for your own feelings: you do not have the right to blame someone else for your reactions even if they may have done something to hurt you. Look behind what has happened, as there may be some emotions that you both have not wanted to deal with. At times, we just need to realise we must accept people warts and all.

Come to terms with the fact that conflict is a natural part of any growing relationship, and, in an argument, decide if you would rather be 'right' or if you would rather have a loving relationship. Arguments are obstacles that can always be overcome.

Never use your love for your partner to manipulate or control them, as this can and will turn on you, according to the natural law of magic and the universe:

A RITUAL TO HELP OVERCOME A BROKEN RELATIONSHIP

You will need to gather:
1 yellow candle
2 pieces parchment (paper)
green ink
2 drops carnation essential oil
2 drops lilac essential oil
1 green candle
a green item of some sort, eg bead, to use as a talisman
heat-resistant dish

Cast a circle of protection around yourself. Then light the yellow candle saying:

'I light this candle to our friendship in love and understanding.'

Sit down and write on the parchment, using the green ink, all your hurt feelings from the relationship. Relive these feelings. When you have finished, sprinkle the paper with the oils. Light the green candle, and hold the green talisman and parchment over the flame. Say three times:

'Let there be love and understanding in (insert both your names) relationship. Let the winds of heaven flow over our problems, and see fit to remove them.'

Place the parchment in the dish and burn it with the flame of the green candle. Scatter the ashes to the wind, and throw the talisman into the ocean, or bury it away from your home.

A Wedding Blessing

Weddings are a time to share love and happiness, not just for the bride and groom but also for the people that attend. A wonderful way to offer newly-weds love and joy is to give the following blessing.

The requirements for this ritual come from many different cultures. The lump of sugar is a Greek custom as is the rice which signifies the blessing 'May you always have a full pantry.' The colour blue is used in many cultures as a symbol of purity, love and faithfulness.

You will need to gather:
something old, to represent the bride and groom's past
something new, to represent the bride and groom's future
something borrowed, to represent the support of others for the couple
something blue, to represent faithfulness
a silver sixpence, to represent prosperity
a lump of sugar, to represent sweetness in the bride and groom's married life
1 cup (250 g/8 oz) rice, to represent fertility

Fill a basket with all of the above, providing a tag for each item to explain what each one represents. Add to this pantry basket home-made jams, chutney, or vinegars etc for the couple's new home. All these goods should be made by you, so that, as you make them, you put your good wishes into them. When the recipients eat or use the items, they experience the love and happiness that has gone into their making.

This basket can also be given as a present for a kitchen tea. Another wedding present can be made from a basket of items for the bedroom. Fill a basket with the following items.

You will need to gather:
2 red candles
1 piece parchment (paper)
love oil (see page 19)
2 glasses, to drink to their life together
love potion (see pages 51-52)
favourite foods or special treats, such as strawberries or pâté

Add to the basket the following blessing, written on parchment, for the happy couple.

PROMISE OF LOVE

This ritual is to be done on your honeymoon.

Put aside a special time and space to perform this ritual. Take the red candles and light them, saying:

'May our love for each other carry us through the sunshine and storms of life.'

Talk to each other about what you want your next year to be like — do you want to travel, to buy a home, or start a family for example. Write down what your desires are and if at all possible do this every year. Take as much time as you need, then with the love oil, anoint each other between the eyebrows and as you do, bless each other saying whatever comes to mind. Fill the glasses with the love potion and look into each other's eyes. Focus on being completely in the moment and drink in silence, for the now is all we have. Seal the blessing with a kiss.

To Draw a Lover

Love potions and love charms are never to be used with force or to demand that your desired partner will fall in love with you. This interferes with the other person's free will, which is against the law of harm no-one. The type of magical charms in this book give blessings that will bring you love in your life as well as giving love for yourself. If your desired person is meant for you, you will create the best possible environment for love to grow in.

The most important aspect to making a love charm is to always know that love comes from your inner love. Reflect on your own love within, as this helps keep the balance and the ritual is then made for your highest good, as well as the highest good of the other person involved.

To have true love in one's life, we must have an inner knowledge of our own love centre, for loving ourselves is the most important part in any love spell. Without that love we will attract a person that is only half of the whole. When we feel complete we attract a person who is also complete, and this is where true love can grow. If we are not complete, we find that another person cannot fulfil our need or their own. It is our responsibility to meet our own needs, no-one else can be there for us if we are not there for ourselves.

When you are involved in creating a love charm, spend some time alone looking at the reasons why you want a lover in your life. Your main reason may be to share your life with one special person or to have someone who accepts you for what you are.

HERBS, OILS, SYMBOLS AND PLANTS OF LOVE

While collecting items for your talisman, absorb the energy of the herb or item and bless each item, as this shows respect for the element that is giving of itself for your talisman. One old Indian tradition is to leave an offering after you take something from nature. This could be a piece of hair or tobacco or any natural product, as fair exchange is important when working with earth magic.

To make your own love pillow, gather together a selection of things that represent love to you. You can include beads, beautiful coloured material such as silk or lace and any other trinkets. Sew these latter onto a small pillow (a ring pillow is good) that you have filled with love herbs (chosen from list below).

Please note: When you are gathering your goodies, make sure you keep your intentions of making a symbol of love. If you take something from nature always put something back in return.

The following is a list of the best plants and herbs to use in making talismans.

ACORNS

APPLE SEEDS: APPLES HAVE LONG BEEN THE FRUIT OF LOVE.

BASIL

BAY LEAVES

CARDAMOM

CINNAMON

CLOVES

COAL

CORIANDER

FEATHERS

GARDENIAS

GINGER

HAZELNUTS: FOR WISDOM

JASMINE

JUNIPER BERRIES

LAVENDER

LEMON

MISTLETOE

ORANGE BLOSSOMS

ORRISROOT

PASSION FLOWERS

PATCHOULI: THIS WAS SAID TO BE USED BY CLEOPATRA.

PERIWINKLE

ROSE PETALS: IF YOU CAN, YOU SHOULD COLLECT ROSES AT MIDNIGHT AS IT IS SAID THAT THESE CONTAIN THE ESSENCE OF LOVE ITSELF.

ROSEMARY

SWEETPEAS

VANILLA

VIOLETS

MAGICAL LOVE BOTTLE
Love in a Bottle

You will need to gather:
1 pink candle
½ cup (30 g/1 oz) rose petals or jasmine
4 cups (240 g/8 oz) lavender
1 tablespoon cumin
wooden spoon
2 drops rose essential oil
2 drops lavender essential oil
rain water (enough to fill bottle)
1 medium bottle

Light the candle and dedicate it to creating a loving environment. In a bowl, place rose petals, lavender and cumin and mix them together carefully with the wooden spoon. Add the essential oils and rain water and combine. Pour the mixture into the bottle, then hold the bottle to your heart. Visualise love pouring into the bottle and charge it with your love by saying:

'Bulbs of love, held in my heart, draw up to me the love I have inside.'

SO MOTE IT BE

Leave the love bottle near your bed so that you will see it every day.

LOVE DRAWING POWDER

This powder can be used as an ingredient in a love charm, or it can just be sprinkled around your home to draw love to you.

You will need to gather:
1 tablespoon ground sandalwood
2 tablespoons ground cinnamon
½ tablespoon dried basil, ground
½ tablespoon talc
2 drops myrrh essential oil
2 drops frankincense essential oil
2 drops rose essential oil
1 piece of red or pink cloth, cut into a heart shape and sewn around
the edges with a top opening left undone

In a bowl, combine all dry ingredients. Add essential oils and mix thoroughly. Place 2 tablespoonsful of mixture into the centre of cloth and sew up. Attach a length of cord to the top of the heart so that you can hang the charm around your neck. This charm can also be hung over your bed or else use the powder to sprinkle in love letters, or around your home or office. This will allow love to fill your world.

acred Chamber Dream Diary Natures Life Force Cast

CHAPTER two LIFE FORCE   *Connect with your essence.*

Life force is the essence of our being. It is the light within our spirit, our health of body and mind, and our outlook on life. When we are ill, it is our life force that is under siege from our thoughts. We all too often let our mental status prevail over our physical wellbeing, so that when we think and feel negative thoughts, we manifest them in our bodies and our lives.

I have often found in my life that when I am ill and things are getting me down, the best help for getting me back on my feet is to use all my knowledge to make myself well. I am the only one who is responsible for my health and when I do get sick it is usually because I have been overworked and have overridden my intuition — I have not listened to my body telling me to slow down. The body does give out signals, but you do need to listen, and this is sometimes the hardest thing of all.

Magic can help you take responsibility for your health by giving you guidance, but this does not detract from the fact that you need to care for your body in the first place. A good diet, exercise and relaxation are all necessary to a healthy body, mind and spirit. After all, you are what you think and feel about.

By creating rituals or blessings for our body and life, we can help to dispel the energies that can and do reduce our life force. You need to forgive yourself for getting sick and not be too hard on yourself. You learn a great deal when things get too hard to cope with, as this is when we can change our life for the better by understanding ourselves and our needs.

Please note: If your illness is serious consult your health practitioner first.

THE TEMPLE OF KNOWLEDGE
A Healing Ceremony

The first step to this ritual is to have a bath. Baths are extremely healing and can be used in all sorts of ways to restore health and balance. The *Healing Ceremony* bath allows the body to open to healing, as water has traditionally been used to wash away negative energies. The most important ingredient in any bath is relaxation.

You will need to gather:
2 tablespoons ground thyme
½ cup (30 g/1 oz) peppermint leaves
¼ cup (15 g/½ oz) lavender flowers
3 drops eucalyptus essential oil
1 green candle

Mix all ingredients together thoroughly and place in a piece of pantyhose. Tie stocking off at the top and put it into a bath of warm water. Light the candle and place it next to the bath. While you lie in the bath, imagine that your body is being flooded with the green healing light. Relax in the warm water and ask your body what it needs to be healed. It may take time to become in tune with what your body requires, but the more you nurture it, the sooner your body will provide you with the answers to your questions. These answers are always within you, however you do need to take time to listen to yourself. When you have finished your bath, take the plug out and imagine that the water is taking away your ills.

Another form of this healing ceremony can be performed outdoors. Find a stream or river of clean water and take off your shoes. Place your feet in the water and feel the water take away the unease from your body. Meditate on your physical wellbeing. Running water helps to purify the spirit and any meditation done at the same time will also help to give you peace within.

Healing a Broken Friendship

Write a letter to your friend's guardian angel and to your own.

You will need to gather:
1 sheet of paper (if you make the paper yourself,
focus on mending your friendship as you make it)
green ink
1 green candle
heat-resistant dish

On the paper write down what you would like the outcome of the ritual to be, for example forgiveness, understanding, or healing. Write your wish while feeling as if it has already been granted. Then ask for guidance from your guardian angel. At the end of the letter write the following 7 times:

will know what is for your highest good. May the angels guide us both to forgive and forget.'

When you are finished, light the candle and place the paper in the heat-resistant dish. Burn the paper with the flame from the candle. Scatter the ashes to the wind and let the wings of the angels take them away.

A BIRTHDAY BLESSING

Traditionally, birthday blessings are very potent. To ask for a wish or to perform a ritual on or around the time of your birthday is very magical. This ritual can be performed with or without the presence of friends.

You will need to gather:
1 white candle
1 green candle
1 red candle
1 piece of parchment or handmade paper
1 medium shell
1 clear quartz crystal
1 cup (250 g/8 oz) salt
a collection of small stones or twigs, or a piece of paper
a journal

Ritual in your life will help keep you connected to nature and to the true nature of your higher self. Before you perform any of these rituals it is best for you to allow enough time so that you may focus on what it is that you want to wish for (follow the *Important Steps to a Ritual*, see page 14).

The first part of this journey is to make a candle dedication, for healing or love. Before you light your candles centre yourself. Centering is done to bring yourself back into an emotional, physical and spiritual balance. Focus on drawing energy into the centre of your body. Sit comfortably and close your eyes to enable you to feel the space around you. This will bring you to an inner stillness.

White Candle dedication: White is for connecting with one's spirit and to provide protection. Light this candle saying:

> *'May the spirit of my wish burn bright.'*

Green Candle dedication: Green is for healing. Light this candle saying:

> *'May my wish always have a firm foundation.'*

Red Candle dedication: Red is for the love of self. Light this candle saying:

> *'May my wish have power.'*

If you wish to carve symbols onto the candles, ensure that you use symbols that hold significance for you.

The best time to make your wish is whilst the candles are burning. On the parchment write down your wish in a positive manner, as if it has already been granted. Then hold the shell in your hands and say:

> *'My wish is held within this shell. May the energy of the ocean grant my wish.'*

Sleep with the shell under your pillow that night. In the morning, take the shell to the sea and throw it into the water. Let the winds of the sea bring you your wish.

Wash the crystal with the salt and leave it to soak overnight. The next day, create a circle around it with stones or twigs, or just draw a circle on a piece of paper and place the crystal in the middle of the circle on the paper. Sit very still and direct all your attention and energy into the crystal. Visualise the crystal glowing with light. To make this crystal yours say the following words:

> *'I now make this crystal mine, I will allow its energy to flow into me, and I will draw energy from it.'*

Leave the crystal in the circle for a few days and when you feel the time is right, place the crystal where you can see it daily or use it in your meditations. This crystal can be used for other rituals.

The next step is to go on a vision quest. A quest is a time spent alone in nature to reconnect with your inner self. It is the best time to ask ourselves questions, and to really listen to ourselves in order to hear the answers. When spending that day alone, do not take anything with you except a journal and some food to eat.

Choose a place in the bush or by the sea, and spend the whole day looking at what is around you. Experience what it feels like to be a tree. Connect with the roots of that tree and ground yourself to mother earth, so that you can listen to what the tree may be telling you. Lie down and look at the sky. Look for shapes in the clouds, and watch the birds. Just by daydreaming you are open psychically, so ask questions and be open to receive messages. They may come to your mind or they may not: the important thing is to be open. You may gain insights but if you do not understand the message when you receive it, do not worry as all will be made clear in time.

TO BECOME CLEARER ABOUT YOUR WISHES, YOU MAY WANT TO ASK YOURSELF THE FOLLOWING QUESTIONS. REMEMBER TO LISTEN TO YOUR RESPONSES.

1. DO I KNOW WHAT I WANT TO DO WITH MY LIFE?

2. AM I DOING WHAT I WANT TO DO?

If you have answered yes, think through your responses and relive what it feels like to be doing whatever you are doing with your life, visualise yourself living it and experience your feelings. If you have answered no, imagine that you are doing what you would really like to do, and ask yourself for details of what it looks and feels like. By doing this you will allow your needs to come to the surface, so you can begin doing it.

Take a journal with you and write down your experiences, so that you will have a record of the day. You may want to take some drawing materials. Do whatever your inner guidance tells you.

To be granted a wish, you need to be certain of what you want, as this is the main reason for performing this ritual. Take as long as you need to complete this blessing, but ensure that it is performed within one complete cycle of the moon.

The Magical Family Heart Share

The purpose of this ritual is to keep a family in open and honest communication, without fear of reprisal or punishment. It also provides the younger members of the family with a means to be heard and a method of communication which they can take out into their lives and other relationships.

Set up a regular time for the family to get together, possibly around the dinner table or whenever all members can be present. If there is a family crisis, or an upset needing urgent clearance, schedule one of these heart shares for the first available opportunity.

Create a sacred space, around a cleared table, or on the floor, whatever suits your family. Create a loving environment. This is a safe place to open one's heart and really tell the truth.

You will need to gather:
4 red candles
1 rose quartz crystal
4 teddy bears, or any other stuffed toys or family mascots
1 red fabric-covered heart filled with some stuffing (for stuffing use love herbs from list, see page 57)

Light the candles and use them to cast a sacred space. Everyone should gather in a circle. Place the candles in a circle with the rose quartz in the centre of the candles. The stuffed toys are to be placed around as you see fit, to provide the feeling that this environment is safe and loving. Lay the heart in the centre of the group. Whoever wants to speak first should pick up the magic heart and start talking, saying whatever comes to mind. This could involve telling another family member something that is bothering or upsetting them. If so, then they should start by explaining what the problem involves, how they feel about it and what they would like to have happen to correct it.

Please note: While a speaker has the magic heart, everyone else listens in silence. Do not start thinking of a response, answer, rebuttal, justification or denial. The aim of this ritual is to allow the speaker to be heard. If the speaker addresses their share to a particular family member, when they have finished, they pass the heart to the one addressed. This person then takes the heart and starts their share with 'What I heard you say was. . . .' This should be the same as what was originally spoken. If it is not, the heart is passed back to the original speaker who has another opportunity to have themselves heard.

The heart can be claimed by anyone who wants to share, or it can be passed around the circle so that everyone has an equal chance to participate. When everyone has finished sharing, take time to hold hands and connect to each other, feeling that all is one. Put the magic heart away until the next family heart share, and remember that any family member can call a family meeting.

This ritual for the family may take time to become familiar and comfortable with, but if you want better communication within your family it is well worth it. Whatever the outcome, you are also working on helping your community: the more work that is done within your family, the more outside people are likely to notice and that will help change our society at large.

WINGS OF A DOVE
Baby Blessing

A new baby in the world is a very special time for all concerned. This blessing can be done with the parents or be done for them.

You will need to gather:
1 white candle
sandalwood essential oil
3 small bells
1 red ribbon
salt
sage leaves

Anoint candle with the oil and charge it with your love and life force. Carve symbols on it that you feel are appropriate. As you light the candle to honour new life, dedicate it to love, health, wealth and success.

Tie the bells together using the red ribbon, with a knot in between each bell. As you tie each knot, give a blessing for love, health and happiness. Then tie both ends together forming a circle of bells. Ring the bells over the end of the baby's bed and say the following words:

'May archangel Michael protect you throughout your life and may love and light guide you always.'

Place the charm at the foot of the bed then sprinkle the salt and sage in the corners of the baby's room in a clockwise direction. As you do this say:

'May only energies that come in love and light be present in this room.'

This can also be done for the rest of the house, if you wish.

✝REASURES ✝O KEEP

PREPARING FOR YOUR BABY

It is time to celebrate your love for each other and welcome your newest family member. Set aside a special time for this blessing, as this time can be very important for both of you to begin bonding with your baby.

You will need to gather:
1 piece of blue silk, cut in the shape of a circle
1 handful dried rose petals (taken from a bunch that was given to you on a special day)
1 handful lavender buds
1 handful white feathers
1 drop frankincense essential oil

1 drop myrrh essential oil
1 blue ribbon
2 white candles
sandalwood essential oil
1 stick rose incense

This charm is a symbol that will surround your child with the protection of your love. You should make this charm when you feel that the time is right. The time nearest to the full moon or the time of a new moon is usually best, as both signify new beginnings.

Mix together the rose petals, lavender buds, feathers, frankincense and myrrh essential oils. Place the mixture on the piece of blue silk. Imagine they are all gifts of love and protection to your new child that are being woven together. Tie this up with the ribbon. Seal the charm with a kiss. Sew a cord to the top of the charm so that each parent can wear it for a week. The charm will then have your energy in it.

Then anoint each of the candles with the sandalwood essential oil. While anointing, charge the candles with your life force. Then light the incense stick as this helps to clear the space for the ritual of blessing the charm.

After wearing the charm for a week each, sit opposite your partner looking into each other's eyes. Connect with your inner guidance, and allow as much time as you need. When it feels right, light one candle each. As you light them state your intentions, visualising your baby with love, health, and happiness. Ask for guidance from your higher self which knows what you as parents need to have and to be for your baby, so that your baby will have all its needs met. Sit and relax and allow the answers to come to you.

Now take the charm and pass it over both flames, making sure you do not burn it. As you do so, say these words together:

'May our child have all its needs met to live its destiny to follow love and light.'

As the candles burn they release the power of your intentions and the smoke takes your blessings into the baby's future. Allow the candles to burn all the way down. Keep the charm in your baby's room.

To rid yourself of habits and behaviours that do not serve you, light a fire of some sort (a candle will do) and sit and meditate before it. Think of all those things you do not need or that are making you unhappy. It may be food so take a portion of that food and throw it into the flames. If it is not practicable to burn the thing itself, then draw symbols of items or feelings you want to rid yourself of on paper and throw the paper into the fire (have a heat resistant dish handy).

This ritual could be done with a few of your friends or alone. Make it a ceremony to celebrating ridding yourselves of non-positive habits. If you wish it can be performed as a service to the planet to stop wars or crises.

Other items that can be thrown into fire as symbolic offerings are rice, seeds or corn, as these represent the seeds of hope.

GIFTS OF THE EARTH

CREATING AN ALTAR IN YOUR HOME OR OFFICE

GOD OR GODDESS ALTAR
A Dedication to Nature

The humble potpourri can be transformed into a magical altar for your home or office. An altar is a place that is set aside for offerings and blessings.

You can use any potpourri you have or you can make your own, and this is where the magic begins.

The following rituals are designed to bring either grounding, protection or love to the environment, so start collecting your precious goodies and put them in your new God or Goddess altar. Dedicate this space to nature spirits who live around you.

FOREST OF DREAMS

You will need to gather:
To add to potpourri: dried leaves (of your choice)
dried flower petals (of your choice)
To make grounding oil: 1 drop basil essential oil
1 drop lavender essential oil
1 drop gardenia essential oil
1 drop thyme essential oil
15 ml (½ fl oz) base oil (either almond, apricot,
avocado or sunflower oil)

Take yourself into the park, or forest, feeling the ground beneath you. Collect goodies like leaves and flower petals, adding them to your forest of dreams potpourri, making the mixture come alive with your magic. This potpourri can be made from any blend of dried herbs and flowers or buy one already made for use in these rituals.

To make grounding oil, blend essential oils with the base oil. To freshen your magical blend add a few drops of grounding oil saying:

'Bring new grounding energies to my forest of dreams.'

ANGEL WINGS

Angel's Love

You will need to gather:
To add to potpourri: 1 feather
dried herbs (of your choice)
dried flowers (of your choice)
To make love oil: 1 drop rose essential oil
1 drop lime essential oil
15 ml (½ fl oz) base oil (either almond, apricot, avocado or sunflower oil)

The angels' love is always around you, and coming across a feather will remind you of their presence. Be on the lookout when you are in the bush or park for feathers of any kind. Place the feather you find in your angel wings potpourri. Potpourri can be made from any combinations of dried herbs and flowers.

To make love oil, blend essential oils with the base oil. To freshen your nest of love add a few drops of love oil saying:

'Guardian angel you are with me for love and guidance.'

This potpourri is for the protection of mother earth and to enable you to feel the connection with it. Feel her protective arms around you, and imagine this nurturing and protection.

You will need to gather:
To add to potpourri: dried twigs (of your choice)
stones
dried herbs (of your choice)
dried flowers (of your choice)
To make protection oil: 1 drop sandalwood essential oil
1 drop anise essential oil
1 drop frankincense essential oil
15 ml (½ fl oz) base oil (either almond, apricot, avocado or sunflower oil)

Add twigs and stones that you find in your surroundings to your potpourri.

To make protection oil, add essential oils to base oil and mix thoroughly. To freshen your magical mix, add a few drops of protection oil saying:

'*You bring to me protection and nourishment.*'

cred Chamber Dream Diary Natures Life Force Cast

CHAPTER THREE PURIFICATION   'Purification is essential to our wellbeing'.

CLEANSING OUR ENVIRONMENTS

Purification of our homes and offices is not only important, it is essential to our wellbeing. Purification will drive away any general negativity in your home. Negativity is the vibration that can come from angry thoughts, negative people visiting your home, sickness, fear, or chaos. Negativity can and does create tension, increase arguments, prevent sleep, and contributes a heavy atmosphere to the home. These unwanted influences can be cleared by purification rituals but they do need to be performed on a regular basis.

Washing with water and cleansing an environment will renew life, for to wash something is a timeless purification ritual.

To rediscover what we really hold to be true and sacred, we must cleanse ourselves and our environments. Clothing is our persona, it is a kind of camouflage which lets others know only what we want them to know. By washing away our personas we allow for purification of the spirit to take place. This is a ritual to weave a new way of viewing our life and situation into our spirits, by making them clean. When cleaning and clearing our homes or offices, we rid ourselves of the old so that the new energy can enter. If your surroundings are feeling weighed down, what you need to do is to clean out drawers and cupboards and throw out things that are taking up room. Make a ritual of it, and when you are finished sprinkle around in the corners of your home or office some loose sage, cedarwood and salt, as they act to clear away the old energy and to protect the new.

Many rituals can be designed for the purification of our homes and lives, the following are just a few. They will help to keep an environment clear so joy and love will have a chance to live and grow.

A seven day candle dedication for a peaceful, loving home.

This seven day ritual is for you to bring the energies of peace, positivity and spirituality into your home or office. For the next seven days or nights you will light a candle and allow it to burn until it is finished. Create an altar around the base of the candle, with crystals, feathers or any other trinkets that feel right for you. The seven candles represent a place of contemplation that goes into the depths of your soul and brings about inner transformation. Lighting the candle symbolises the guiding light of your higher self. In numerology, seven is a spiritual number, having the vibration of spirit surrounding it.

You will need to gather:
7 candles
7 crystals, feathers or stones or a combination of these

Begin the ritual by creating a protective space by casting a circle. The circle is made by visualising white light surrounding the area you are sitting in. This helps keep the space clear of unwanted energies. Ask only for energies that have healing or positive work to do for you.

Before lighting the candle, contemplate what your dedication will be then take a sharp object and carve into the candle the desired symbol. Remember to use a symbol that means something to you. As you carve the symbol, send your energy into the candle and charge it with your intention and life force.

Once you have carved a symbol into the candle, take a few minutes to clear your mind and be ready to visualise what it is you need. While visualising, light the candle saying:

'I dedicate this candle to peace, love, harmony, positivity and spiritual awareness.'

Repeat this ritual for seven days running, changing the dedication as you see fit.

A RITUAL FOR A PEACEFUL HOME

You will need to gather:
1 handful jasmine
1 tablespoon honey
2 passion flowers
1 handful white rose petals
½ cup (125 ml/4 fl oz) spring water

For a peaceful home, mix together all the ingredients. As you blend them, visualise your home or office being filled with love and light. Place the mixture in a jar where you will see it everyday.

THE WELL OF FORGIVENESS

You will need to gather:
red ink
1 piece of paper
a small jar
vinegar (enough to fill the jar)

To enable you to forgive someone who has wronged you, write their name nine times with red ink on the piece of paper. Place the paper into the jar and cover it with the vinegar. Secure the jar and throw it into a river or ocean, or bury it away from your home.

TO REDUCE DISQUIET

This spell it to rid the house of any disquiet or agitation.
You will need to gather:
1 black candle
1 white candle

Light the black candle and say:

'*May all the negative energy from this problem burn away as this candle burns.*'

Allow the candle to burn all the way down and then bury the remaining part stating:

'*Let all the remaining negative energy be transmuted into the ground.*'

Once you have done this, light the white candle and say:

'*Our home is full of love and light so mote it be.*'

Allow the candle to burn out.

A SACRED SANCTUM

PURIFICATION SWEEP

You will need to gather:
a piece of string
4 rosemary branches
4 fennel branches
1 white candle
¼ cup (60 g/2 oz) rock or table salt
cedar essential oil

Please note: The use of four symbolises all types of change for the better.

Use the string to tie together the rosemary and fennel branches to form a small broom. As you tie them together, focus your intention on sweeping your home or office clear of any tension, bad vibes, and anger. It is important to keep focusing on charging the symbols you are using with your personal energies so that you work with the energies to purify your environment.

Light the candle and sprinkle around the base of it a circle of salt saying:

> *'This salt purifies this space.'*

Dedicate the candle to holding in all the love and light by anointing it with the oil. Walk around the rooms of your house sweeping over your possessions, always keeping the focus on your intention. Then go to the doors outside your home or office and whisk all the energies out. Do this for as long as you need to.

When you have finished, dispose of the broom in a reverent manner, thanking the spirit of the plants for their help. Either bury it or put it in the garage outside the house. Do not throw it away or burn it, as this shows disrespect.

LIVING WATERS

Bathing is one of the oldest forms of relaxation. It takes your mind off the worries of the day and baths can also be used to bring about love and joy. These bathing rituals are a great way to purify your thoughts and mind.

A SACRED JOURNEY
Pearls of Wisdom Bath Ritual

The purpose of this ritual is to provide the space for some deep and healing communication to happen between you and your intimate partner. This is a very powerful process to affirm one's love or to clear any upsets or crises in a relationship.

Set up a time when you want to be in close and totally honest communication with your intimate partner. Alternatively, if you have a great itch to get something out into the open, set aside a time at the next available opportunity. Take the phone off the hook, switch on the answering machine, and put aside the outside world during this special time for yourselves.

Create a safe, magical space in your bathroom for some healing work together. Have lots of candles (using colours of your choice), sensual love oils (see page 19) and crystals available, which will add to the power of this ritual. Place the candles and crystals around your bathroom, and use the love oils in the bath water. Remember to have plenty of flowers decorating your sacred space. Consider also the possibility of having some wine or champagne handy!

Get into the bath together and sit facing each other. Whichever partner feels the need starts first by saying:

'What I feel like saying is. . . ' (or some other appropriate start).

Then the first speaker proceeds by detailing the problem and how they feel about it. They then finish by saying:

'And what I love about you is. . . ' and tell their partner what that is.

The first speaker continues until they have nothing else left to say. The other partner listens and totally receives their mate's communication without response of any sort. Both partners take it in turns to speak out until they are totally replete and have cleared the problem and spoken their truth. Each person needs to feel they have been totally received by the other.

Healing a Rift in a Relationship

Take a bath to heal a damaged relationship, and while soaking in it concentrate on healing the rift. Prepare the space in your bathroom, and have as many pink and red candles as you feel you need around the room. Make sure you will not be disturbed.

You will need to gather:
1 handful jasmine
1 handful rosemary
1 handful carnation petals
1 handful lavender buds
1 sprig mint
fluffy towel, prewarmed

Mix all the herbs together and place in a piece of stocking or pantyhose. Tie the stocking off at the top and place in the water. Leave this in the bath while you soak. Visualise that the rift is over and relax in the soothing water for as long as you need to. Dry yourself with the towel.

Redo this ritual for as long as the rift is still around.

THE TIDES TURNED

Success in Business or Career Bath
You will need to gather:
3 tablespoons marigold flowers
3 tablespoons mint
3 tablespoons parsley
3 tablespoons fennel
3 tablespoons nasturtium flowers and leaves
1 green candle

Combine all the herbs and flowers in a piece of stocking or pantyhose and tie it off at the top. Place the stocking in the water, and leave it there while you soak. Light the candle and gaze into the flame, saying:

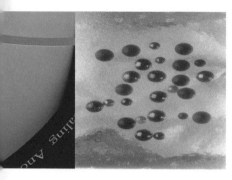

*'I shall bathe
and I shall be
as green and strong
good herbs, as thee
draw me favour
draw me fame
draw bright honour
to my name (say your name)
so mote it be.'*

The following is a list of other herbs for the bath.

BAY LEAVES: COMFORT AN ACHE IN THE LIMBS

CHAMOMILE: SOOTHING AND RELAXING

ELDER LEAVES OR FLOWERS: HEALING AND STIMULATING

LAVENDER: REFRESHING

LIME FLOWERS: CALMING

MUGWORT: RELIEVES TIREDNESS

FAVOURABLE DAYS FOR BATH RITUALS

MONDAY: BATHS TAKEN PRIOR TO SLEEP SECURE PROPHETIC DREAMS

TUESDAY: INCREASES PASSION

WEDNESDAY: STRENGTHENS THE INTELLECT

THURSDAY: BRINGS MONEY YOUR WAY

FRIDAY: HELPS YOU TO FIND LOVE

SATURDAY: BRINGS PATIENCE

SUNDAY: MAKES YOU STRONGER AND HEALTHIER

BEST TIMES FOR BATHS

MORNING: INCREASES BEAUTY

NIGHT: ENHANCES PSYCHIC AWARENESS

NOON: INCREASES LUCK AND FORTUNE (ESPECIALLY IF TAKEN AT THIS TIME DURING A FULL MOON)

acred Chamber Dream Diary Natures Life Force Cast

CHAPTER FOUR MAGICAL PANTRY   *A cupboard filled with magic.*

The magical pantry is an assortment of magical rituals with miscellaneous uses. This section contains rituals, spells and blessings that cover a wide variety of needs and desires.

FINDING LOST ITEMS

To find a lost item, draw it on a piece of paper. While you draw it, focus on seeing the item coming back to you. Place the drawing into your magic box (see below), and wait until the answer comes to you. If this does not happen, ask why it was lost and listen to the answer. Write the name of the lost item on a piece of paper and pin it to a pillow or cushion and leave it there until you find it.

Sit down, clear your mind and ask for inner guidance to help you locate the item you have lost. Look back on the last time you saw the item and retrace your steps. For best results, do not force the process — it will come back to you even without you ever worrying about it. If the item does not return to you, you will know to let it go as it was not meant to come back. Remember that someone else may need it more than you.

To make a magic box, follow these instructions.

You will need to gather:
1 old cardboard box
paint
pictures (of your choice)
material, for lining

Using an old box is the easiest way to make your own magic box. Paint or cover it with pictures, in a special design. Line the inside with the material and you can then use it to find lost items. A magic box can also be used to grant wishes. Write down in a focused way what you need, and then place your wish into the box. Wait on the will of heaven for your wish to be granted.

To grieve is to heal: it is a process that is natural and healthy, and it is a very important rite of passage. It is our own individual perception and interpretation which designates what is loss and each person will have their own way of dealing with it.

When there has been a death in your life the hardest part is letting go of the departed. Grief can also be finishing a relationship, someone you love going overseas, or your child leaving home: all are important so by acknowledging the grief you are on your way to healing it. When you feel it is time to let go, you can start to use the releasing grief beads. These grief beads can also be made for another person.

You will need to gather:
18 coloured glass or clay beads
a piece of cord or string

Take the cord and tie a knot at one end. Start to string the beads one by one. As you do this experience yourself feeling peaceful or meditate. Meditation is merely time spent within, so make each bead represent a mantra. A mantra is a prayer to bring about the healing of the spirit. Say the following mantra for each bead you place on the string, or make one up of your own.

'I am love and the light within heals me.'

When you have strung all the beads, take the beads and sit alone and allow yourself to feel. Being aware of your feelings will help you in the healing process, as they give you the strength to carry on. In time you will need to let go of the attachment and let your heart feel less heavy as you lessen your burden of grief.

Meditate for the same amount of time each day, even if only for a few minutes, with the beads, and use them to help keep in touch with your feelings. You may want to throw the beads into the sea one by one, or bury them, once you feel your grieving is over.

YES/NO STONES

You will need to gather:
2 flat stones
paint

To make these stones, simply paint the word 'yes' on one stone and the word 'no' on the other. You can start using them straight away. Please note: Do not ask questions such as 'Should I go up this road?'. Use the stones as you would use any divination tool, to guide you through the storms of life.

Place the stones in a bag or lay them face down and shuffle them around. Hold a question in your mind, and draw out one stone, or turn one over, to reveal the answer.

A STONE'S THROW
Helping Release Anger

You will need to gather:
a piece of amethyst crystal

Go to a river or the ocean. Take the piece of amethyst to the water's edge and sit down. Feel your anger welling up inside you and channel that energy into the amethyst. Do this until you feel the stone fill up with your anger. Then, with all the force you can handle, throw the stone into the water, then say thank you to the river or ocean for allowing you to release your stored up anger. Turn around and walk away without looking back. Feel the calmness you now have inside you.

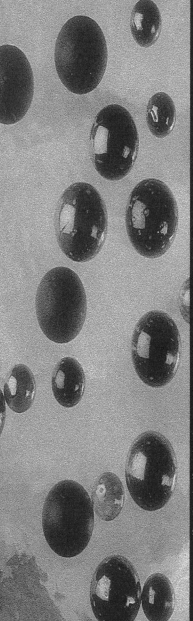

Writing in your dream diary will help you to deal with everyday problems, by creating a record of recurring symbols that will help you to look for patterns in your dreams. This allows you to analyse consciously the events in your life that are being presented to you in your dreams. They provide insights to what you should be doing to overcome unwanted worry in your life.

The power of a dream symbol is that they are so close to the very essence of life. Their meaning tends to remain constant. You are the only one to know what each symbol means to you. There are some common meanings but you do not have to use these. Symbols access a hidden centre within ourselves, and they can also be used for meditation in a quest for inner peace and spiritual wisdom.

DREAM ARROW

You will need to gather:
1 stick of hard wood
1 penknife
sanding paper
assorted coloured ribbons

Take a stick or piece of wood and shape the top with a knife, so that it looks like an arrow. You may want to sand the wood, if so then as you sand think of the dreams you want to come true and charge the arrow with them. When you have finished sanding you could carve in the stick the symbols that represent something to you. Tie coloured ribbons on the stick and hang it above your bed and let the arrow catch your dreams.

A WISHING POD

You will need to gather:
a seed pod from any tree (acacia or gum) or an eggshell
1 piece of handmade paper (it is best if you make your own)
pictures to represent your dream

To make your dreams come true, take a pod of any tree or use an eggshell. On a piece of handmade paper write down what the dream is and decorate this with pictures you have cut out. Make sure that you put your intention behind what you want by making it as real as possible. Place the paper in the pod or shell and bury it in a young pot plant or a new tree. Now let the wish go and wait on the will of heaven.

HOPI INDIAN PRAYER FEATHER

This prayer feather can be made by one person or the whole family. Have everyone collect feathers to use.

You will need to gather:
1 red feather, for the south
1 black feather, for the west
1 white feather, for the north
1 yellow feather, for the east
1 piece of red string
1 piece of black string
1 piece of white string
1 piece of yellow string

These colours represent the four directions of protection. Take the pieces of string and tie the feathers together with them. As you tie the feathers, focus on your intention of love or joy.

Hang the prayer feathers in a place that everyone will see every day. This ritual can be redone every year with new feathers; or you can just add new feathers to the original.

A HELPING HAND

This ritual is for a friend needing a little help and support. This person needs to do this ritual for themselves.

You will need to gather:
1 red candle
3 drops love oil (see page 19)
1 purple candle
a piece of jade, for luck

Anoint the red candle with the love oil, keeping a focus on love and success. Then light it and say the following words:

'I dedicate this candle and space to love and success.'

Then take the purple candle and anoint it and dedicate it the same as the red candle. Hold the jade in your non-writing hand and fill it with your life force and your intention of love and success. Place the jade in front of the candles as this helps to charge the crystal. When candles have burnt out completely you will have the jade to use as a talisman for your intention.

A ritual for welcoming a new house-mate.
You will need to gather:
1 yellow candle
1 bottle of red wine or other drink
1 cake (bake it yourself if you can with the intention of living well together)
1 stone or crystal

Arrange a dinner for the new person, and place on the table the candle, wine, cake and stone, before you start the meal. All the household should be present and seated. Ask everyone to close their eyes and have one house-mate start by casting a circle. Ask someone else to light the candle and say out loud:

'I dedicate this candle for our home to be filled with joy and happiness.'

Then take the stone and pass it around. Each person should make a statement regarding what they would like their life together to be like, such as to have all disagreements cleared up quickly and without anger, etc. Place the stone somewhere you can all see it, as this will remind you of your agreements, then start the dinner and finish with the cake. Each person should have a piece, to symbolise their joint respect for each other.

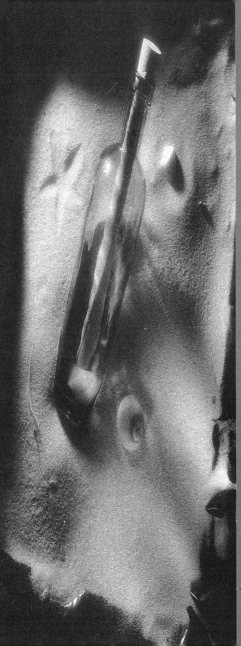

Today most health food shops, new age book stores and a
few gift stores carry all of the items listed in this book. Some
of the items may also be found in your supermarket, such as
candles and dried herbs. Pure essential oils are best bought
from health food stores or new age book stores. Look for
companies that specialise in natural products.

DRAGON'S PARLOUR (QVB)

Magic by Mail
Level 2, Shop 27, Queen Victoria Building, George Street,
Sydney NSW 2000 Australia
Providores of herbs, oils, crystals, magical candles,
books and magical products.
Please write for a mail order catalogue.

EARTH'S NATURAL WONDERS

Lower Ground, Shop 55, Queen Victoria Building,
George Street, Sydney NSW 2000 Australia

Ames, Kenneth & Jones, Julia 1992, *Love Potions*, David Porteous, Devon.

Atwood, Mary Dean 1991, *Spirit Healing Native American Magic and Medicine*, Sterling Publishing Company, New York.

Buckland, Ray 1993, *Practical Color Magick*, Llewellyn Publications, Minnesota.

Cabot, Laurie & Cowan, Tom 1992, *Love Magic, The Way to Love Through Rituals, Spells, and the Magical Life*, Dell Publishing, New York.

Campanelli, Pauline 1992, *Wheel of the Year Living the Magical Life*, Llewellyn Publications, Minnesota.

Cavendish, Richard (ed.) 1987, *Mythology, An Illustrated Encyclopedia*, Macdonald and Co.

Cirlot, J. E. 1993, *Symbols, A Dictionary*, Redwood Books, Towbridge.

Cunningham, Scott 1993, *Earth Power, Techniques of Natural Magic*, Llewellyn Publications, Minnesota.

Cunningham, Scott 1993, *Encyclopedia of Magical Herbs*, Llewellyn Publications, Minnesota.

Cunningham, Scott 1993, *Living Wicca, A Further Guide for the Solitary Practitioner*, Llewellyn Publication, Minnesota.

Cunningham, Scott 1992, *Magical Aromatherapy, The Power of Scent*, Llewellyn Publications, Minnesota.

Cunningham, Scott 1993, *Magical Herbalism*, Llewellyn Publications, Minnesota.

Cunningham, Scott & Harrington, David 1993, *Spell Crafts Creating Magical Objects*, Llewellyn Publications, Minnesota.

Cunningham, Scott 1993, *The Complete Book of Incense, Oils and Brews*, Llewellyn Publications, Minnesota.

Cunningham, Scott & Harrington, David 1992, *The Magical Household*, Llewellyn Publications, Minnesota.

Cunningham, Scott 1993, *The Truth About Herb Magic*, Llewellyn Publications, Minnesota.

Daniel, Alma, Ramer, Andrew & Wyllie, Timothy 1992, *Ask Your Angels*, Ballantine Books, United States.

Estes, Clarissa Pinkola 1992, *Women Who Run With the Wolves, Contacting the Power of the Wild Women*, Rider, United Kingdom.

Fontana, David 1993, *The Secret Language of Symbols, A Visual Key to Symbols and Their Meanings*, Pavilion Books, London.

Hope, Murray 1991, *Practical Atlantean Magic, A Study of Science, Mysticism and Theurgy of Ancient Atlantis*, Aquarian Press, London.

Johnson, Robert A. 1989, *Ecstasy, Understanding The Psychology of Joy*, HarperCollins.

Jones, Julia 1992, *Love Tokens*, David Porteous, Devon.

Line, Julia 1992, *Discover Numerology, Understanding and the Using the Power of Numbers*, The Aquarian Press.

Loader, Rhea 1990, *Dreamstones, Magic From the Living Earth*, Prism Press, Great Britain.

Marlborough, Ray T 1993, *Charms Spells and Formulas*, Llewellyn Publications, Minnesota.

Nahmad, Claire 1993, *Lovespells, The Authentic Collection of a White Witch*, Pavilion Books Limited, London.

Paulson, Genevieve Lewis, *Kundalini and the Chakras*, Llewellyn Publications.

Richardson, Alan 1992, *Magical Gateways*, Llewellyn Publications, Minnesota.

Slade, Paddy 1990, *Natural Magic, A Seasonal Guide*, Hamlyn Publishing, London.

Telesco, Patricia 1993, *A Victorian Grimoire*, Llewellyn Publications, Minnesota.

Tisserand, Maggie 1990, *Aromatherapy For Women*, Thorsons, London.

Tisserand, Robert B. 1977, *The Art of Aromatherapy, The Healing and Beautifying Properties of the Essential Oils of Flowers and Herbs*, C. W. Daniel Company Ltd, England.

Willis, Tony 1991, *Discover Runes, Understanding and Using the Power of Runes*, The Aquarian Press.